The Unknowable Mystery of Other People

Sally Zakariya

A Publication of The Poetry Box®

Editing & Book Design by Shawn Aveningo Sanders.
Cover Design by Robert R. Sanders.
Author Photo by Mohamed Zakariya

ISBN: 978-1-948461-13-9
Printed in the United States of America.

Published by The Poetry Box®, 2019
Beaverton, Oregon
ThePoetryBox.com

Contents

The
Unknowable Mystery
of
Other People

Treavor Times Three

1. After Easter

Thank you sir, thank you ma'am. He smiles
as we press a few bucks in his hand.
Treavor owns this corner, stands here rain or shine
with his crutches and his Combat Veteran sign,
leans back against the curved steel traffic guard,
takes the weight off, waits for somebody to stop.
Desert Storm destroyed his legs, the V.A. failed
to fix them, still he jokes with his regulars.

How was your Easter? he asks us when we stop. *Fine,*
we say, but we don't make much of the eggs and cross.

*My parents were killed Easter morning on the way
to church,* Treavor tells us. *Back then my folks
were healthy, good for their age. Walked every day.*

He frowns. *The drunk who hit them, he survived,*
he says. *Easter's hard for me.* As if the rest was easy.
But now another regular pulls up, and Treavor smiles.

2. Change for a Funeral

No black man's gonna bury my momma,
Treavor says, *that's what she told me,
only she used a different word.*
He's talking about the Appalachian
woman who shared his spot and how

her family turned its back on her—didn't
even visit when she lay dying in the hospital.
I went there every day—she was my friend.
He looks down. *Folks give me change,* he
says, *and I save it up in those big water jugs.*

Years of nickels, dimes, and quarters—
enough to pay for his friend's funeral,
enough to see her safely in the ground,
see her safely in the hands of the Lord.

*Her daughter didn't care. She's got six
kids, all Bible names—some Christian.*

The light goes green. We hand Treavor
a few dollars and wish him a good day.
We drive on, wondering if we've
really done our Christian best.

3. Nobody Knows

I'm not afraid to die, he says. *No gun
scares me now, not after Desert Storm.*

Sun slanting in on his angular dark face
Treavor has another story to tell.
*He pushed a gun right at me—like I
had something to steal. Did you see
it in the papers? I told the cops
and the reporter. I told them I'm
not afraid—nobody knows but God.*

It's easy to think God has deserted him but
he holds on—like his sign, Always Faithful.

*God knows everything, he says, knows
how many hairs are on your head.
If you've got too many trials and
tribulations, he'll take you early.*

Treavor straightens, adjusts his crutches,
looks up. *I'm not afraid.*

The Iranian Artist Explains

Everything starts from zero, he says.
We start with nothing but an urge
and then a bare duality of dot and line
    of black and white
            of sound and silence.
Consider the sequence of creation—
    note measure melody
            letter word text.

Calligraphy and music—he joins them
    for us here in the gallery.
Listen to this line from Rumi, he says
pointing to a piece beside him on the wall
singing the long sweet glide of one letter
    the round note of another.

Outside the August air trembles
    with storm.
Thunder cracks, lightning flares.

There is meditation in the practice, he says
in the daily repetition of pen on paper.
There is spirit in the work, he says,
and the skies reply, showering down
    on the eager earth.

The Seer

Which is better, 2 or 3, 3 or 4? she's switching lenses
in the Steam Punk apparatus on my face *which is better?*
as a cloud of unknowing obscures the eye chart's type.

Round steel-rimmed lenses the retro glasses on a comic book
anarchist—F E L O P Z D so small but perhaps the anarchist
might read this line before he throws his bomb.

We talk about vision, the eye doctor and I, about mysteries
of light and life, this wise woman, bespectacled herself
and with a seer's knowledge of the future.

I always knew that I'd have Asian kids, she tells me,
speaking of her two adopted children from Korea, *ever
since I was thirteen I knew* she says, switching lenses.

Which is better, 4 or 5, 5 or 6? Which is better, to see
or not to see, to know or not to know, to throw the bomb
or not to throw it? My eyes begin to water.

*And once I woke up knowing that the plane would crash
so I refused to board* she tells me *even though I've never
been afraid of flying and yes it went down over Pittsburgh.*

Which is better, the anarchist's bomb or the plane crash?
F E L O P Z D still defeats me and my eyes still water.
Which is better, to know what's coming or to wait and see?

Their Desserts

Robin, who couldn't hide her innocence, maker of poppy
seed cake, unhappy in love, leaning toward the nunnery
      last I heard

Jeanne of the freckles and flaming orange hair, never quite
one of our group and remembered mostly for her
      carrot cake

Willie, practical Midwesterner who did it all a year ahead
and better, who served flaky almond pastry from her
      Dutch forebears

friends and family all filed together in the old recipe box
under Cakes and Cookies along with others—Mother's
      there of course

no baker, still we relished her peach skillet pie and apple
goodie, sweet memories neatly recorded in her own left-
      leaning hand

Nancy, too, big sister who settled into a domesticity I envied
but failed to emulate (I never make her pecan pie but savor
      the recipe)

and you, Aunt Betty, your spice cake topped with tangy lemon
sauce deserves a poem of its own, warm and pungent, starting
      with the same

simple stuff as all the rest—flour, butter, sugar, eggs—
but how various the cooks, how various their desserts

Aunt Betty's Spice Cake

Oldest sister and least pretty
tall and raw boned and awkward
and forthright, she always knew
the right way to get things done

The right way to make a spice cake:
plenty of cinnamon and cloves
and nutmeg along with sugar
and eggs and the foundational flour

I can almost hear her recite the recipe
in her Eleanor Roosevelt voice—
you gels she would call my sister
and me and it wasn't an affectation

She married an Army man who died
too young, and thoughtless child
that I was, I never saw her sorrow
only her no-nonsense certitude

Aunt Betty I make your cake
for you and top it with rich lemon
sauce from the cookbook you
gave me when I married

Love Letter from a Fire

For my mother, who told the story

She hoped to catch some breath of air that hot summer night
but it was greasy smoke that pushed through the screen
bringing with it the first notes of a Chopin nocturne

Three houses down flames raced up walls ... devoured the roof
left beams burned black ... scored deep ... rough as tree bark
blazing embers shot small comets across the sky

On the lawn a man sat at a scorched piano ... pajamas
soot-smudged ... fingers finding solace in familiar keys
flames reflected in the sweat that shone on his forehead

Years later when she heard Chopin the acrid smell
would come back to her ... the sight of a piano saved
from fire ... the unknowable mystery of other people

Mr. Moxley

No kids of their own, they let us roller skate
up and down their broad smooth driveway.

I'd see her smiling from the porch as we rolled by
and Mr. M. would wave when he came home,
a dark square sort of man who always wore a cap
and clutched a dome-lid lunchbox.

One summer day we heard sirens screaming down
the street.
> *He shot himself,* my mother said.
> *In the head,* my friend told me.

I made a paper basket and left it filled with flowers
at Mrs. Moxley's door.

I couldn't shut the picture out—blood streaming,
screaming red like fire sirens.

Out of the Gutter

*He pulled me out of the gutter
so many times,* he says, harsh
voice demanding our attention.

Maybe he should have left you,
I think uncharitably, not really
meaning it. But we've already
heard his life story, schmearing
our bagels a table away, heard
how he was thrown out of one
college for drugs and drink.
How his dad flew cross country
to bail him out for DUIs. How
each time they went out
for beer and bonding.

*We're Irish—we're all drunks
but we don't talk about it,*
he says, talking about it, talking
so loudly half the diner hears.

I'm in the program now, he says,
*go to bars with friends but I don't
drink.* Maybe he's the AA sponsor
for the two guys with him, done
eating but dawdling over coffee.
Why else would two 50-something
men listen so intently to a loudmouth
half their age?

I like to tell my story, he says.
My dad does too.

Everyday Blessings

She would stand at the sink
singing hymns
elbow deep in dishwater
baptizing each plate with suds
glory glory praise be
no matter the meal
the food was blessed
and we who ate were blessed

She would rock in her chair
on the front porch
back and forth and back
humming the hymnal
darning socks
praise be
blessed be needle and thread
blessed be socks
and the feet that wear them

Her blessings flowed out
to tomatoes on the vine
sparrows in the oak tree
tomcat by the back door
clouds overhead
neighbors passing by

Somewhere somehow
she's still there on that street
of my childhood
washing dishes
darning socks
dispensing her blessings
praise be

Leaving Eden

Black silk hair, summer dresses
they leave the Vietnamese store side by side
a grandmother with a grocery bag
　　　　lemongrass fish sauce rice
a mother with a yellow stroller cradling
the round-cheeked hope of the future

Another dynasty in the making
another prayer in Missionary Catholic
or the East Asian triple religion
　　　　Buddhist Confucian Taoist
another scholar, government official
anybody's guess, but most of all
another bearer of the filial promise
to revere the ancestors

Our promise was special forces
was agent orange, was Mi Lai
was Little Saigons coast to coast like this one
just outside the nation's capital

Eden Center with its Buddhist temple arch
its Good Fortune supermart
its restaurants and mini-malls
its flag of what was once South Vietnam

Mother and grandmother leave Eden Center
bringing a little bit of Vietnam home

Memphis Manicure

Twenty fingers between us, we waltz in,
two old Anglo ladies with time on our hands.

What do you think of us as you snip and buff
and polish? What do you think of our entitled lives
as you sing like birds in your six-tone tongue?

At lunch time do you think of lemongrass
and sticky rice and the spicy *larb* of Laos
or of the ribs and grits and whiskey here
in your adopted home where the Wolf
and Mississippi meet?

Trading your land of tropical monsoons
for this humid Southern city, leaving family
and friends—have we, in our smug First World
way, welcomed you and made your journey
worth it?

I try to see myself in Vientiane, too large,
too pink, all out of place—a reckless,
careless being—while you, so neatly small,
so deft and economical, bring fleeting beauty
to my foreign fingertips.

A Gift over Coffee

Coffee and poetry and friends—
the two of us meet regularly,
and this time we've got the café
almost to ourselves.

It was her idea—this younger,
smarter, more successful writer –
her idea to workshop our work,
to lend a second ear and eye.

She wields her pen like a sculptor's
chisel, shaping and slicing away the fat
that builds up when my fingers
get lazy on the keyboard.

That's no problem for my friend,
who writes straight, spare lines
on loss and the uncompromising
grief it carries in its wake.

She knows these subjects well,
knows the anger and despair,
the clueless things that people say,
the hard constancy of it all.

Today, though, we hear giggles
from the next booth, infectious
laughter from a gaggle of young
girls not yet tinged with sorrow.

But we're intent on rescuing my poem,
which has strayed far from its path.
Why not try this, she says, *or this,*
turning a deft phrase or two.

She who has lost so much herself
yet has so much to give.

Hospital Lobby

I've been to all of them, he says,
rocking back and forth, arms
wrapped around himself, *every
shelter in the city,* naming
them one by one, intoning
like a Biblical prophet
in a B movie. *All of them.*

Everyone looks away, away
from this embarrassment
in frayed sweatpants and bedroom
slippers. *Every single shelter,*
rocking harder and deeper
like water coming to a boil.
*All I want is money for the bus,
money and something to eat.*

It takes a hospital official, brisk
in suit and badge, to lead him
away, promising a hot cafeteria
meal. Everyone is pleased.
Smiles of satisfaction. Problem
solved. Embarrassment gone.
*I can't make it on my own out
on the street,* he says, but
now no one is listening.

Requiem for a Nobody

Unknown, unsung, no obituary
to spell out the bare facts of his life,
just one of the many to perish alone
on the street, hand still outstretched
for help that would not come.

Lord have mercy on his soul,
his nameless soul.

Death knew his name, called him by it,
called him from an indifferent world
where he slipped by mostly unseen,
wrapped in a tattered gray blanket.

Death found him where he waited,
cheeks fallen in, eyes dimmed,
invisible to people bustling by.

Once someone tied his shoes, held
his hand, kissed his baby cheek,
but there will be no Pieta for him.

Lord have mercy on our souls,
our oblivious souls.

When We Lived on R Street

You could have been anything with your olive
skin, your black hair cut too short to see the curl

When your white mother split from your black father
(jazz musicians both) she took you to Paris

where life was easier for folks like you and when
you came back you could have been anything

You could talk street or you could talk French
but my mother said to me, *your Father wouldn't like it*

My father from the white pillared house that cotton built
who was a fair man, a kind man,
                              but still

He would have admired your music, I like to think
and your Continental manners
                              but still

What would he have made of his blue-eyed girl living
with this man who could have been anything but was
in this country, at that time
                              nothing but black

Valedictory for G.

They're playing jazz in heaven

No more missing out on promotion at the library
though you know more about recorded sound
    (the spooled wire, the reel to reel)
than the white man with all his degrees

No more seeing your father on the street
    slumped, mumbling, rheumy eyed
the price of a short dog all he asked
all he asked of you for years

No more seeing your light-skinned daughter just
once a month
    having to beg for even that

The women you cared for don't forget your soft voice
how the dark hairs corkscrewed into your chest
how you lit candles by the bath in the third-floor walk-up
    (a different time, and long ago)

They're playing jazz in heaven now
    Art Tatum, John Coltrane, and the rest
        cigarette-smoke clouds
ham steak and macaroni on the table
your ulcer healed—miraculous recovery

Praise be to the music

The Mystery You Sought

You were lost twice over
first to the guru we called a charlatan
then to the alluring ledge
where you either fell from grace or leapt
toward something like transcendence
leaving your wife and year-old son
to wonder why, wonder how to live
with sorrow and with guilt they had no call
to feel.

What I remember are the marigolds and fruit
heaped on the stage around the leader
when you took us to a meeting early on
also the sweet empty gaze of the believers
how they pressed around us hungrily
murmuring welcome chants in the dim light
as if we'd come to join them, not to find out
for ourselves.

What I remember is how we'd scoff
and try to bring you back to the young man
you'd been before, bring you back
to the man with everything to live for—
everything, at last, but the dark mystery
you sought.

The Girl Who Memorized Her Father

For B., daughter of Holocaust Survivors

In case he went away and didn't come back
in case they took him and put someone else
in his place—such things happened in books
didn't they and in the old bad times
before he came to America

So she studied him and learned his every
detail—the length of his fingers, the breadth
of his palm, the texture of his skin,
the awkward slope of his shoulders
one higher than the other

She watched the way he walked
down the hill from the subway
every night—the length of his stride
the slight forward angle of his body
as though he couldn't wait
to get home to her

They can't imitate a walk she thought
they can put on spectacles and grow
a moustache but they can't fool
someone who knows your walk
or the way your hair grows in a V
down the back of your neck or
the network of little lines around
your eyes or the exact tone of your
voice when you say *I'm home.*

To an Obituary Writer

Every day a thousand deaths—nameless,
uncounted, unremarked on—allies,
enemies, strangers.

The earth groans under its anonymous
burden of hidden lives, bone
on unknown bone.

Every day you resurrect the dead and introduce
them to us one by one, unfamiliar,
unacknowledged until now.

The inventor no one's heard of, the unsung
composer, the one who survived disaster
beyond imagining.

Over coffee I give them their small due
of sorrow, someone I wish I'd known,
then tomorrow someone else.

To a Monk on Wisconsin Avenue

Washington, D.C.

Unfathomable, set apart
with your tonsure and robe,
your poor man's rope belt echoing
the circle of your hair, you stand
in stillness as a host of ordinary
mortals rush by.

Grave, serene, like an old statue
of a saint, you seem somehow
suffused with an almost visible
aura of goodness, of otherness,
a shield against temptation,
against evil.

Tell us, Friar, what are we to make
of the poor and frightened,
the victims of hate and greed?
All the secular power in this most
worldly of cities, all the quarrels
and posturing, have not found
the answer.

To the Accordion Player Outside Whole Foods

You conjure whole geographies of tune
Scottish moors, streets of Tijuana, hills
    of Italy

Rattle of grocery carts
    children's shrieks
        dusty parking lot
all dissolve as your fingers find their way
from song to song around the globe

Few shoppers stop and fewer still toss
    coins into your hat
but I am caught by melody
forgetting apples, milk, and cheese

I am lifted out of dailyness
taken up, transported by your chords
    and trills
let the shopping go—while you play
    I'll listen

Women in Their Summer Hats

Broad brims shield their indoor faces
from summer sun and my eyes,
but I know these women
       or women like them.

Past young but still nowhere near old,
they congregate in like-minded groups
to walk the weight off after lunch.

Arrayed in summer-flower colors,
water bottles at the ready, they're two abreast,
a group of six in ritual procession
       down the street.

They cut a wide swath through the crowd,
brims wielding a circular sort of clout—
not the gentle sway of garden party straw
but the firm authority of early cardinals'
       wide-brimmed red hats.

At a busy corner, one pauses to assess
the traffic, raises her hand in a gesture
       of seeming benediction,
then dips her head, her hat's flat disk
angled sharp against the sun.

I picture the six of them spinning away—
plates on a celestial juggler's sticks,
their conversation spiraling
       in prayer.

The Watchmaker's Wife

Attuned to the rhythmic conversation of gears,
she has come downstairs to wind the clocks
before the hour strikes.

Carved longcase clocks, keywound mantel clocks,
railway station clocks, she knows their names,
their histories, their maladies.

But that's his world. Her world began an ocean over,
her work not tied to time, her eyesight halved
by childhood injury.

Today a watch has died, hands frozen still
at quarter after one, band frayed and torn.
Single-eyed, she resurrects it.

One eye's enough. She nods, hair falling
past the one that doesn't see. *It happened
long ago. I compensate.*

Mr. Lee's Watch & Clockworks says the sign
outside the shop. Inside, the watchmaker's wife
minds clocks, makes time work.

What I Know about Chemistry

Grandfather was a chemist but the science
gene died with him in the Maine woods.

Hiker, archer, fisherman, consummate
outdoorsman, but still always a chemist

pursuing the central science. I see
him white coated with his test tubes

exploring the essential secrets
of the universe, matter's mysteries

how atoms meet and dance and bond
in shapely mathematical precision.

I can't fathom such formidable beauty
can't grasp the fundamental knowledge

he held so easily. Did he see molecules
in dreams, devise arcane reactions as he

walked from home to lab, from lab to home?
Samuel Stockton Voorhees—I look in vain

for some suggestion of his sibilant name
in the periodic table. But never mind.

When he was young, I'm told, he saved a man
from drowning in the Johnstown Flood

no doubt analyzing the murky mixture
of flood water and debris as he dove in.

The Memphis Aunts Make Ravioli

Along the length of a well-scrubbed wooden table
Aunt Lil and Aunt Lou lay out a ribbon of pasta

Everything here is old, including Lil and Lou
graying hair in identical buns
print housedresses capaciously aproned
sensible old-lady shoes
stockings rolled to the knee

> *We drove down to Memphis in the old*
> *Plymouth, first trip to Dad's home town*
> *first visit to his family and the cousin*
> *I fell in love with on the spot*
> *my first crush, black-haired Clay*
> *who bought me my first banana split*
> *creamy wondrous sweet syrup of love*
> *a summer of firsts*

Striding down the table Aunt Lil dots the pasta
with savory dollops of ground meat
Aunt Lou rolls out fresh dough for the top
crimps it down between each mound of filling

I eye the little hills ranged neatly in pale rows
waiting to be parted by a fluted pastry wheel
eased into a boiling bath, then lovingly
swaddled in a blanket of tomato sauce
no cans, no boxes, just food by hand
my first glimpse of what real making's like

Hoarder, with Orchids

He collected newspapers and magazines
    years of them
bright spines of *National Geographics*
stacked high like a yellow brick road
    to the sky
piles and piles of publications carefully
curated wall by paper wall
narrow pathways between those walls—
a tantalizing maze to me at six

He was my parents' friend
and later they said he'd gotten worse
but he seemed fine to me—
a builder, an excavator creating
his own topography there in his
    living room
an archaeologist who could find
history at the bottom of each mound
even if he couldn't find a clear space
    for Mother to sit

But he made room for his orchids—
lavish flourishes of blossom
pink to lavender to blue arrayed
    in graceful sprays
lovingly tended in a big bay window
row by row, a sort of orchard
with a generosity of empty space
    between the plants

The Giant Next Door

Gigantism in Ireland from ancient gene, scientists reveal.
~ ScienceWorldReport.com

How tall is a giant? Eight foot four
some claimed for the famous Irish giant
Charles Byrne—tall enough to be
the toast of London two centuries ago.
Crowds came to gawk.

No fairy tale, though Ireland has plenty
of such tales—and plenty of real giants,
thanks to a mutant gene. A pituitary tumor
made Bryne goliath, scientists found later.
He died young.

Did my neighbor have a tumor too?
Did he share that quirky Irish DNA?
All I know is that his great head grazed
the clouds, or seemed to.
I was six.

Black hair, big jaw, coke-bottle glasses.
He was so tall his legs refused to fit
in any ordinary car. Instead he drove
a touring car seized from a gangster,
bought cheap at government auction,
a car with an ooga horn to warn us:
a giant is coming.

Did he die young? So many real-life
giants do. And there was something
sad about him, Mother said, and shook
her head. But what I remember is the thrill
when he let me ride on the running board
        or sound the horn.

He disappeared. Not died, I hope.
At least not then. Moved away,
I'd like to think, to Ireland,
        land of giants.

A Memory of Madness

She's twirling in the middle of the street
lacy black skirt swirling up around her
belting out the blues, her cigarette-whiskey
voice carrying down the block

Cousin Barbara the Crazy One, and how
I envy her abandon, how I love her song
love her fancy party skirt and it's
only the middle of the day

But it won't do
The family is appalled
It's not the first time
It won't be the last

We visit her at St. E's, doors locked
windows barred, walls a sorrowful
shade of green that casts a sour
tint on Cousin Barbara's face

No singing, no twirling
Her eyes are dull

She's long gone now, but mornings
when I take my own mood pills
I remember Barbara—her wild
joy that day, her frantic beauty
and then the awful emptiness
of her eyes

God and Noodles

For M., an Islamic calligrapher

Sunday you sit down to lunch with God—
at least the voice of God—an intimate
meal, just you with a film crew of 16,
plus Morgan Freeman, who's come
to interview you for his TV show.

Not just God's voice but God's gentleman,
you tell me—this fine, warm Delta man
sitting next to you at the Thai restaurant,
where you talk about God and movies
and old-time rhythm and blues.

At home you show him how you write
Allah, another of God's many names.
The crew catches the scratch of reed pen
on burnished paper, the golden tracery
illuminating words of praise.

Complex by design, your calligraphy
twins word and thought with beauty,
like the Thai chef fuses nourishment
and taste in noodles any god would
savor—sustenance for body and soul.

Acknowledgments

I am grateful to the following publications, in which these poems first appeared, sometimes in slightly different forms:

Between the Lines: "To a Monk on Wisconsin Avenue"

Boston Literary Magazine: "What I Know about Chemistry"

Foliate Oak Literary Magazine: "To the Accordion Player Outside Whole Foods"

Glass Poetry Journal: "The Iranian Artist Explains"

Kindred: "The Memphis Aunts Make Ravioli"

Nous: "After Easter " ("Trevor Times Three," part 1)

Panoplyzine: "Everyday Blessings"

Ponder Review: "Their Desserts"

The Poet's Domain (Live Wire Press): "To an Obituary Writer"

The RavensPerch: "The Seer" and "Women in Their Summer Hats"

Women's Voices Anthology (These Fragile Lilacs Press): "Hoarder, with Orchids"

When You Escape (Five Oaks Press): "When We Lived on R Street," "Valedictory for G," and "The Mystery You Sought"

Notes

Regarding the poem, "Treavor Times Three" on pages 9-11, Treavor has founded a nonprofit organization, Falls Church Values Veterans, which provides assistance for homeless and injured veterans and those suffering from PTSD and other mental and physical problems. If you, or anyone you know, might benefit from this assistance, please visit the website: https://www.fallschurchvaluesveterans.org.

Praise for *The Unknowable Mystery of Other People*

Sally Zakariya's *The Unknowable Mystery of Other People* is a revelation. The elegant poems in this collection are each small but vividly drawn portraits of unique characters, from the disabled veteran begging coins to pay for his friend's funeral, to the Aunties baking their distinctive cakes and pies, to the Islamic calligrapher lunching with Allah. And every portrait tells a story—and a truth. We see the famous Irish giant towering above us when she writes: "Black hair, big jaw, coke-bottle glasses./He was so tall his legs refused to fit/in any ordinary car." And we glimpse something of the soul of the watchmaker's one-eyed wife when Zakariya tells us: "Today a watch has died, hands frozen still … /Single-eyed, she resurrects it." Even for the "Nobody," "Death knew his name, called him by it." What seems unknowable becomes known, and the reader cannot help but find the mystery and the humanity in each of her varied subjects.

~ Charan Sue Wollard, author of *In My Other Life*
and *The Magician's Wife*

With spare but select words, Sally Zakariya reveals the essence of a person and transforms often-ordinary experiences of life into vital vignettes. On the lawn outside a smoldering house "a man sat at a scorched piano … pajamas/soot-smudged … fingers finding solace in familiar keys." Of a homeless vet accepting coins at the intersection she notes "Desert Storm destroyed his legs, the V.A. failed/to fix them, still he jokes with his regulars." Her poetry moves from existential questions arising during an

[…]

eye exam to sweet memories revealed between lines of cake recipes—on each page, witnessing the extraordinary potential often lying just below everyday encounters.

~ Rebecca King Leet, *Living with the Doors Wide Open*

About the Author

 Sally Zakariya has been writing all her life—articles, fiction, poetry, random notes and lists. She lives with her husband and two cats in Northern Virginia, where she studies poetry and Spanish and writes at an antique desk looking out at telephone wires and maple trees. Her poetry, which has appeared in some 70 print and online journals, has been nominated for the Pushcart Prize and Best of the Net and won prizes from the Poetry Society of Virginia and the Virginia Writers Club.

Zakariya is the author, most recently, of *Personal Astronomy* (Finishing Line Press) and *When You Escape* (Five Oaks Press). Her other poetry books include *Insectomania* and *Arithmetic and other verses*, both from Richer Resources Publications, for whom she serves as part-time poetry editor. In 2015, Zakariya conceived, edited, and designed an anthology of culinary verse, *Joys of the Table*.

A former magazine writer and editor, Zakariya has designed and self-published illustrated alphabet books on anatomy, food, literature, and other topics. She blogs at www.butdoesitrhyme.com.

About The Poetry Box®

The Poetry Box® was founded by Shawn Aveningo Sanders & Robert R. Sanders, who wholeheartedly believe that every day spent with the people you love, doing what you love, is a moment in life worth cherishing. Their boutique press celebrates the talents of their fellow artisans and writers through professional book design and publishing of individual collections, as well as their flagship literary journal, *The Poeming Pigeon*.

Feel free to visit the online bookstore (thePoetryBox.com), where you'll find more titles including:

Giving Ground by Lynn M. Knapp

Broadfork Farm by Tricia Knoll

The Poeming Pigeon: A Literary Journal of Poetry

Psyche's Scroll by Karla Linn Merrifield

November Quilt by Penelope Scambly Schott

Fireweed by Gudrun Bortman

Shrinking Bones by Judy K. Mosher

14: Antologia del Sonoran by Christopher Bogart

Painting the Heart Open by Liz Nakazawa

Epicurean Ecstacy by Cynthia Gallaher

and more . . .